PIANO   VOCAL   GUITAR

UNEXPECTED SONGS

22 Songs by Lyricist Don Black

ISBN 0-634-05813-4

HAL•LEONARD®
CORPORATION
7777 W. BLUEMOUND RD. P.O. BOX 13819 MILWAUKEE, WI 53213

Visit Hal Leonard Online at
www.halleonard.com

Preface

Ever since I began walking around the magical streets of Broadway I have had this fantasy that one day I would have a book to go alongside the books of Johnny Mercer, Sammy Cahn, Stephen Sondheim, etc. Songwriters have always been my heroes. For me, Oscar, Larry, Ira, Irving, Cole and the rest deserve to have statues erected and postage stamps issued in their honour.

A properly honed lyric is as satisfying to my ears as a Beethoven symphony. Getting a lyric to be just right is a very tricky, almost indefinable, mind-bending challenge. I once compared it with doing your own root-canal work. The British playwright Christopher Hampton said it was like wrestling with elephants.

I have been enormously lucky in working with some of the most brilliant composers in the world. It's impossible to name them all, as there are over one hundred of them! My varied list of collaborators came about because I have somehow managed to straddle the worlds of pop music, movie songs and musical theatre. That is the reason why some of the following composers seem like strange bedfellows: Andrew Lloyd Webber, Quincy Jones, Charles Aznavour, Jule Styne, John Barry, Mort Shuman, Henry Mancini, Charles Strouse, Michel Legrand, Frank Wildhorn, Elmer Bernstein, Jim Steinman, etc., etc.

The one thing that all these people have in common is that they are all searching for the same thing when they are at the piano—a great tune. And every time I begin a lyric I am looking for some fresh way to say something just a little bit differently. When I first heard Oscar Hammerstein's "Fish gotta swim, birds gotta fly, I gotta love one man till I die," I was hooked. The simplicity, the compression, the emotion—it just got to me. And although I have written over eight hundred songs, I haven't wavered in my search for some kind of condensed eloquence.

This book covers a period of almost forty years of lyricwriting, from "Born Free" (1967) to *Dracula* (2003). In between, we have some James Bond theme songs, songs from Broadway and West End shows, and songs from the movies.

I am enjoying writing my lyrics as much as I ever did. Like Ol' Man River, I intend to keep rolling along.

—Don Black

CONTENTS

4   AMIGOS PARA SIEMPRE

10   AS IF WE NEVER SAID GOODBYE (FROM *SUNSET BOULEVARD*)

22   BEN (FROM *BEN*)

26   BORN FREE (FROM *BORN FREE*)

19   DIAMONDS ARE FOREVER (FROM *DIAMONDS ARE FOREVER*)

28   IF I NEVER SING ANOTHER SONG

38   IS NOTHING SACRED

31   THE JOURNEY HOME (FROM *BOMBAY DREAMS*)

44   LOVE CHANGES EVERYTHING (FROM *ASPECTS OF LOVE*)

54   THE MAN WITH THE GOLDEN GUN (FROM *THE MAN WITH THE GOLDEN GUN*)

49   NEXT TIME YOU FALL IN LOVE (FROM *STARLIGHT EXPRESS*)

58   ON DAYS LIKE THESE (FROM *THE ITALIAN JOB*)

64   PLEASE DON'T MAKE ME LOVE YOU (FROM *DRACULA*)

61   SAM

68   SHAKALAKA BABY (FROM *BOMBAY DREAMS*)

75   TELL ME ON A SUNDAY (FROM *SONG AND DANCE*)

100   THUNDERBALL (FROM *THUNDERBALL*)

80   TO SIR, WITH LOVE (FROM *TO SIR, WITH LOVE*)

84   TRUE GRIT (FROM *TRUE GRIT*)

88   UNEXPECTED SONG (FROM *SONG AND DANCE*)

92   WITH ONE LOOK (FROM *SUNSET BOULEVARD*)

96   THE WORLD IS NOT ENOUGH (FROM *THE WORLD IS NOT ENOUGH*)

AMIGOS PARA SIEMPRE
(Friends for Life)
(The Official Theme of the Barcelona 1992 Games)

Music by ANDREW LLOYD WEBBER
Lyrics by DON BLACK

Gentle habañera feel

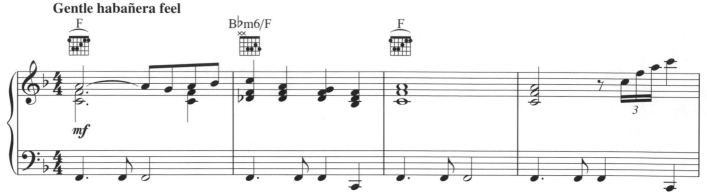

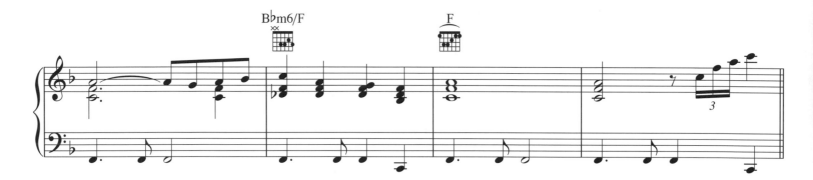

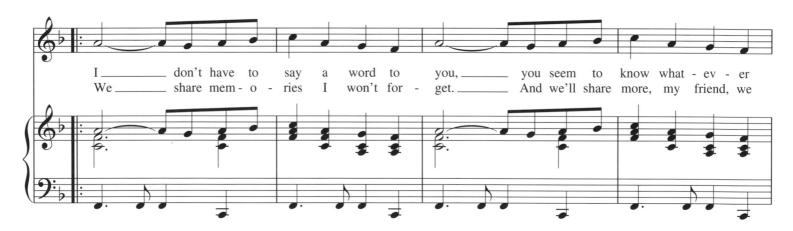

I _____ don't have to say a word to you, _____ you seem to know what-ev-er
We _____ share mem-o-ries I won't for-get. _____ And we'll share more, my friend, we

mood I'm go-ing through. Feel as though I've known you for-ev - er.
have-n't start-ed yet. Some-thing hap-pens when we're to-geth - er.

You _____ can look in - to my eyes and see _____ the way I
When _____ I look at you I won - der why _____ there has to

Gm/F   B♭m6/F

feel and how the world is treat - ing me.   May - be I have known you for - ev -
come a time when we must say good - bye.   I'm a - live when we are to - geth -

F   B♭   C9

- er. }
- er. }   "A - mi - gos pa - ra siem - pre" means you'll al - ways be my friend. "A - mi - gos pa - ra

F   Dm7   Gm
                                                        3fr

siem - pre" means a love that can - not end. _____ Friends for life, not just a sum - mer or a

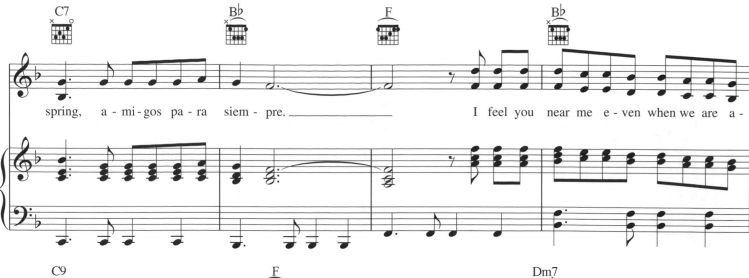

spring, a-mi-gos pa-ra siem-pre. _____ I feel you near me e-ven when we are a-

part. Just know-ing you are in this world can warm my heart. _____ Friends for

life, not just a sum-mer or a spring, a-mi-gos pa-ra siem-pre. _____

Maestoso

When _____ I look at you I won - der why _____ there has to come a time when we must say good - bye I'm a - live when we are to - geth - er.

"A - mi - gos pa - ra siem - pre" means you'll al - ways be my friend. "A - mi - gos pa - ra

rall.

a tempo

8

siem - pre. _____ "A - mi - gos pa - ra siem - pre" means you'll al - ways be my

friend. A - mi - gos pa - ra siem - pre means a love that can - not end. Friends for

life, not just a sum - mer or a spring, a - mi - gos pa - ra siem - pre, a -

mi - gos pa - ra siem - pre. _____

AS IF WE NEVER SAID GOODBYE

from SUNSET BOULEVARD

Music by ANDREW LLOYD WEBBER
Lyrics by DON BLACK and CHRISTOPHER HAMPTON,
with contributions by Amy Powers

but I'm not in an-y hur-ry, _____ and I

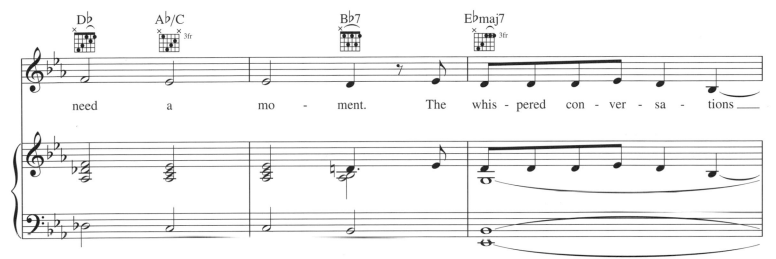

need a mo-ment. The whis-pered con-ver-sa-tions _____

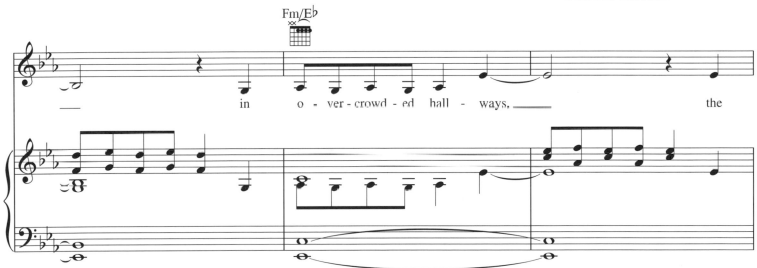

in o-ver-crowd-ed hall-ways, _____ the

at-mos-phere _____ as thrill-ing here _____ as al-ways. _____

Feel the ear - ly morn - ing mad - ness, _____ feel the mag - ic in the mak - ing. _____ Why, ev - 'ry - thing's as if we

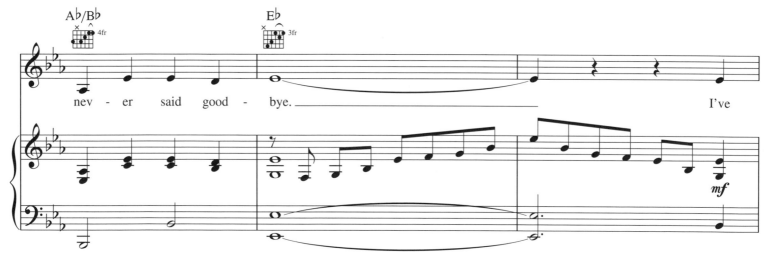

nev - er said good - bye. _____ I've

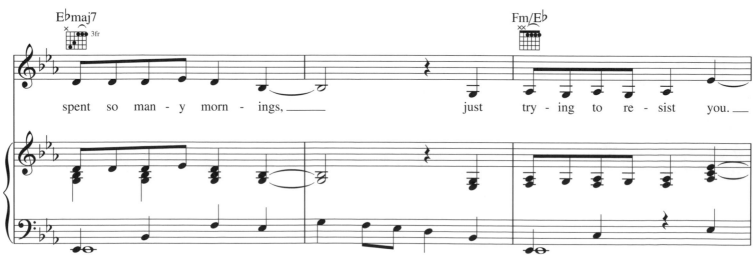

spent so man - y morn - ings, _____ just try - ing to re - sist you. ___

I'm trem - bling now, __ you can't know how __ I've

missed you, _____ missed the fair - y tale ad - ven - tures __

__ in this ev - er - spin - ning play - ground. _____ We were

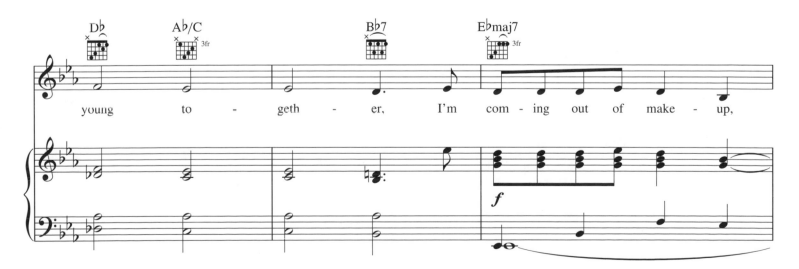

young to - geth - er, I'm com - ing out of make - up,

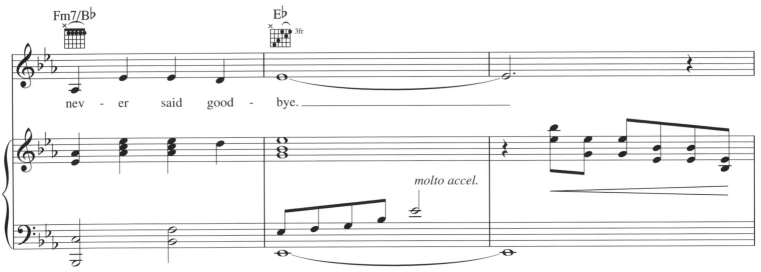

nev - er said good - bye. _____

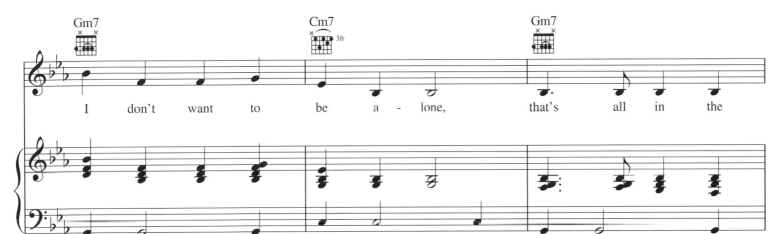

I don't want to be a - lone, that's all in the

past. This world's wait - ed long e - nough, __

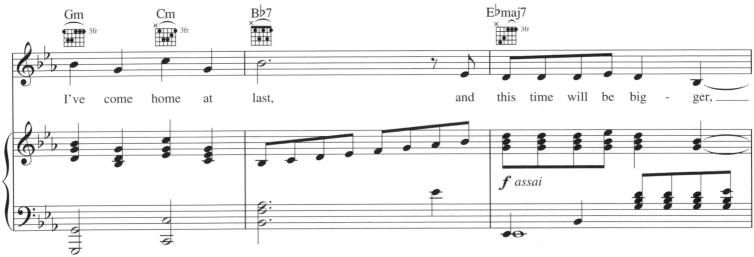

I've come home at last, and this time will be big - ger, ___

and bright-er than we knew it. _____ So

watch me fly, ___ we all know I ____ can do it. _____

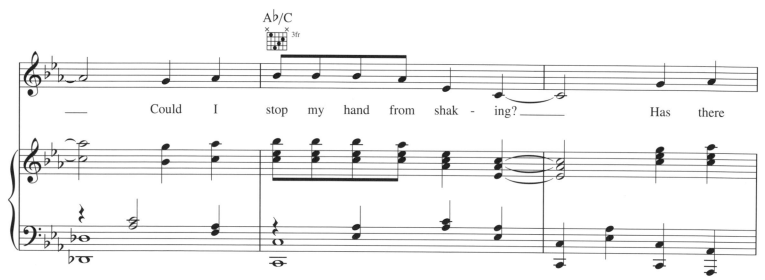

___ Could I stop my hand from shak-ing? _____ Has there

ev-er been a mo-ment _____ with so much to

live for? The whis - pered con - ver - sa - tions _____ in

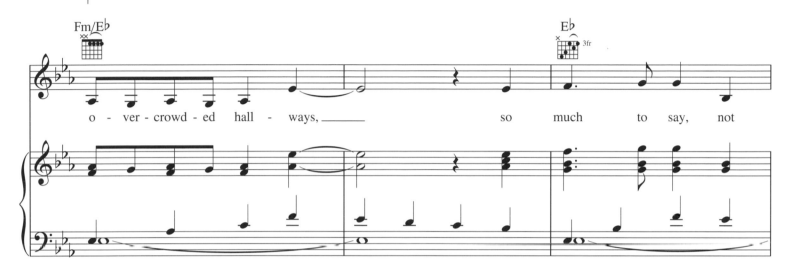

o - ver - crowd - ed hall - ways, _____ so much to say, not

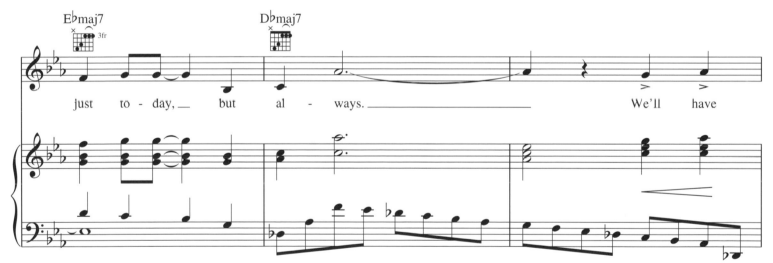

just to - day, _ but al - ways. _____ We'll have

ear - ly morn - ing mad - ness, _____ we'll have mag - ic in the mak - ing, _____

DIAMONDS ARE FOREVER

from DIAMONDS ARE FOREVER

Words by DON BLACK
Music by JOHN BARRY

Moderately (♩ = 104)

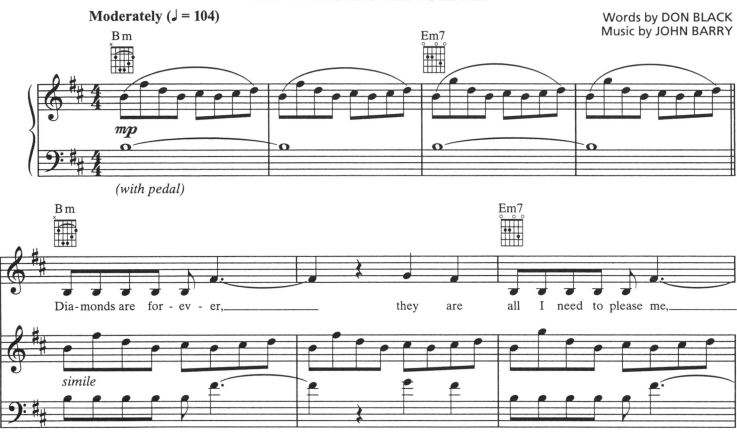

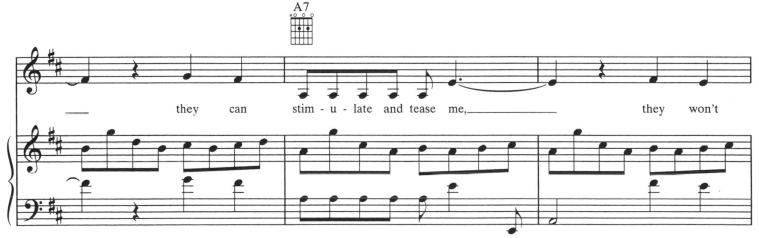

Dia-monds are for-ev-er,_____ they are all I need to please me,_____ they can stim-u-late and tease me,_____ they won't

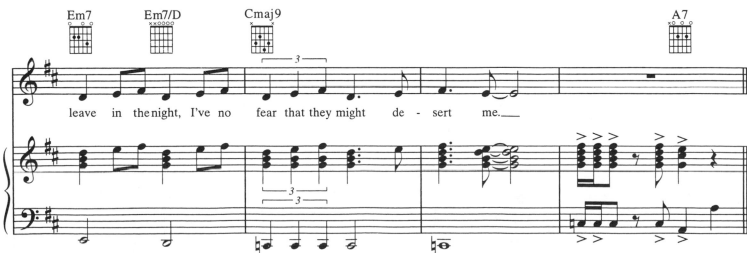

leave in the night, I've no fear that they might de-sert me._____

BEN

from BEN

Words by DON BLACK
Music by WALTER SCHARF

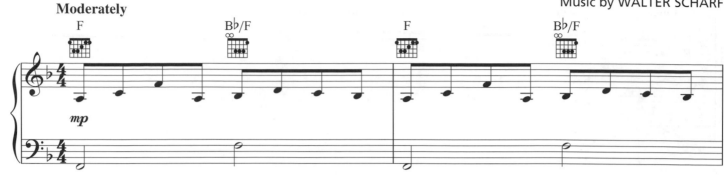

Ben, the two of us need look no more. We both found what we were

look-ing for. With a friend to call my own, I'll nev-er be a-

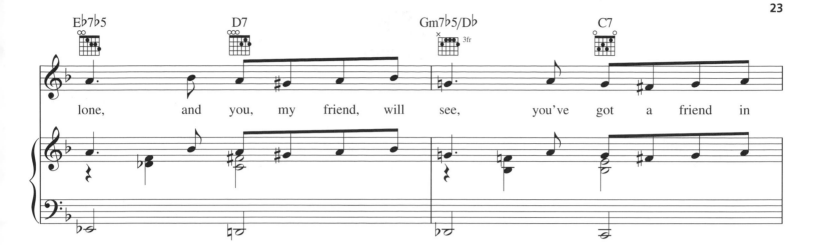

lone, and you, my friend, will see, you've got a friend in

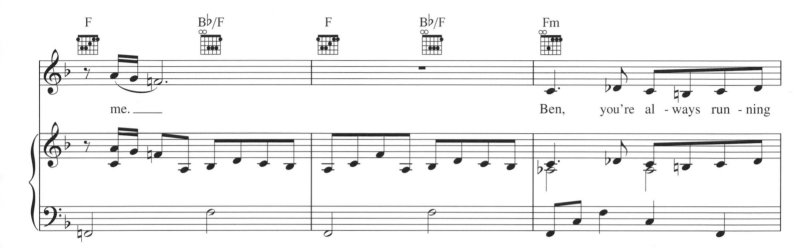

me. _____ Ben, you're al-ways run-ning

here and there. You feel you're not want-ed an-y-where.

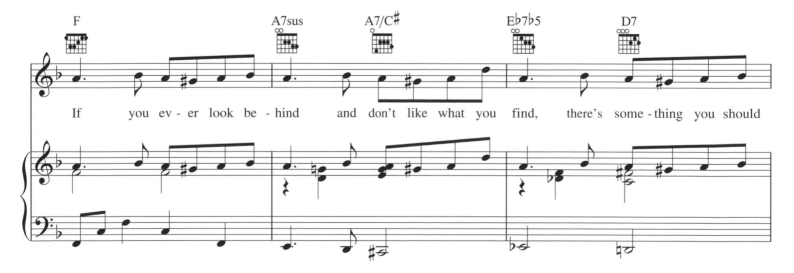

If you ev-er look be-hind and don't like what you find, there's some-thing you should

24

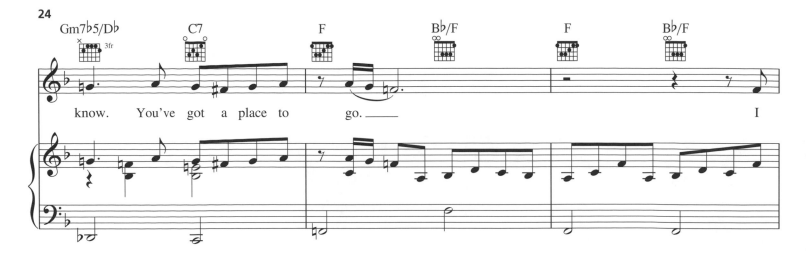

know. You've got a place to go. _____ I

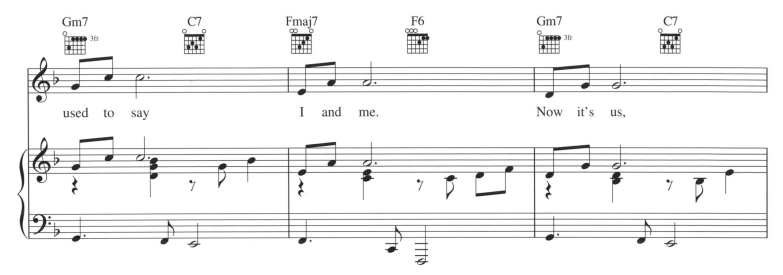

used to say I and me. Now it's us,

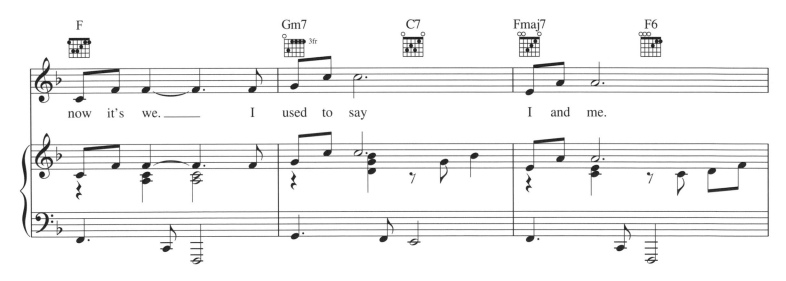

now it's we. _____ I used to say I and me.

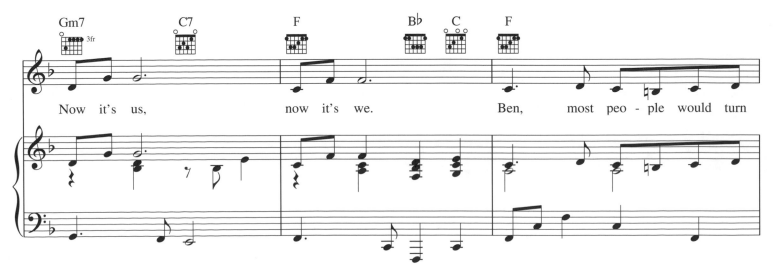

Now it's us, now it's we. Ben, most peo - ple would turn

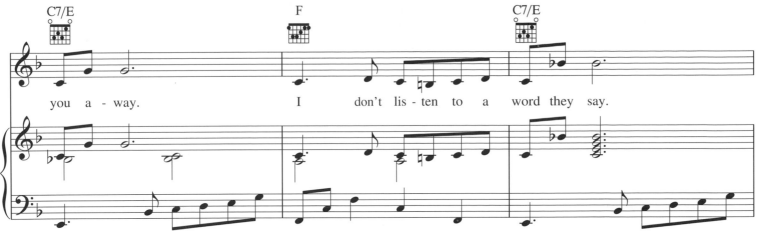

you a-way.   I don't lis-ten to a word they say.

They don't see you as I do;   I wish they would try to.   I'm sure they'd think a-

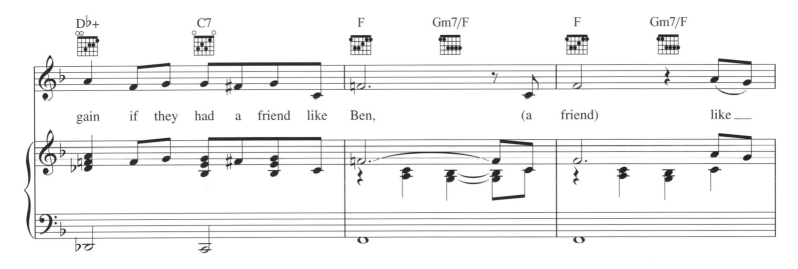

gain if they had a friend like Ben,   (a friend)   like

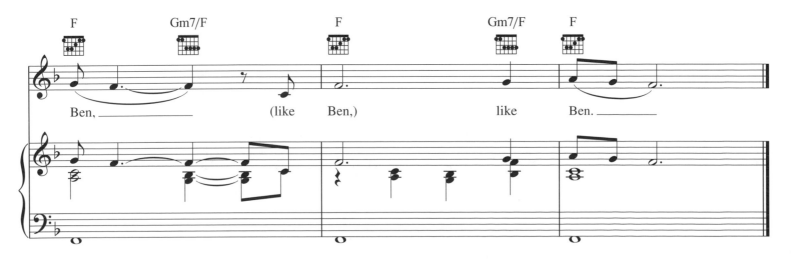

Ben,   (like Ben,)   like   Ben.

BORN FREE

from the Columbia Pictures' Release BORN FREE

Words by DON BLACK
Music by JOHN BARRY

Stay free, _____ where no walls di - vide you, _____ you're free as a

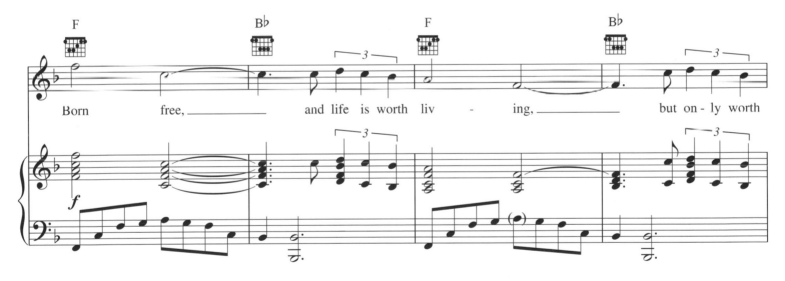

roar - ing tide, so there's no need to __ hide. _____

Born free, _____ and life is worth liv - ing, _____ but on - ly worth

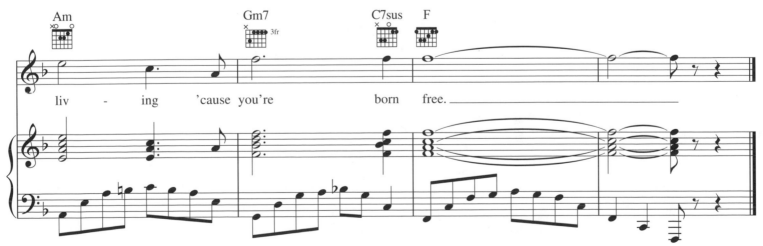

liv - ing 'cause you're born free. _____

IF I NEVER SING ANOTHER SONG

Words and Music by DON BLACK
and UDO JURGENS

THE JOURNEY HOME

from BOMBAY DREAMS

Music by A.R. RAHMAN
Lyrics by DON BLACK

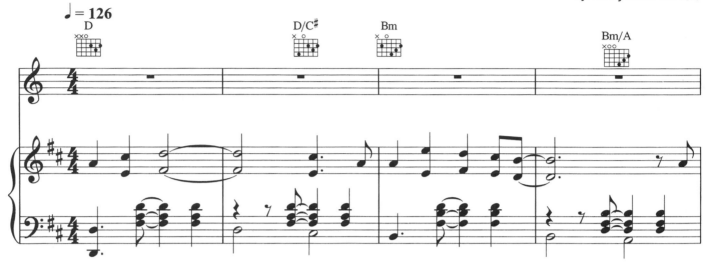

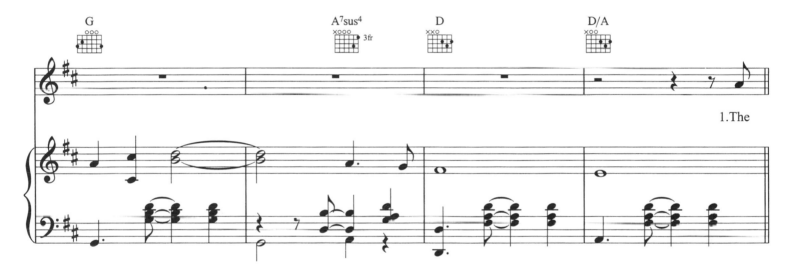

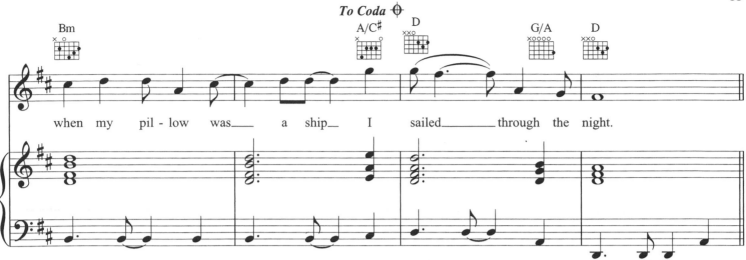

when my pil-low was___ a ship___ I sailed___through the night.

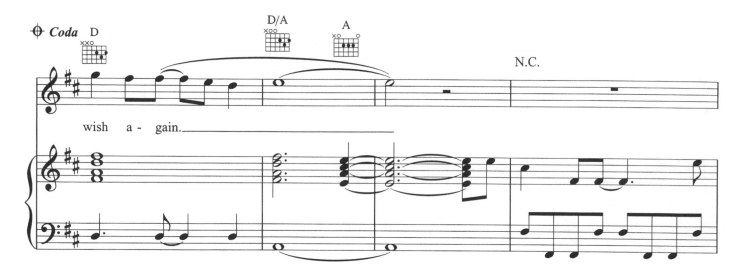

wish a - gain._____

Not ev - 'ry road__ you

come a - cross__ is one you have__ to take.___ No,

some - times stand - ing still can be__ the best move you ev - er

be - fore the train.

Vocal ad lib.

poco rit.

Verse 2:
The journey home is never too long
When open arms are waiting there
The journey home is never too long
There's room to love and room to spare
I want to feel the way that I did then
I'll think my wishes through before
I wish again.

IS NOTHING SACRED

Words and Music by DON BLACK
and JIM STEINMAN

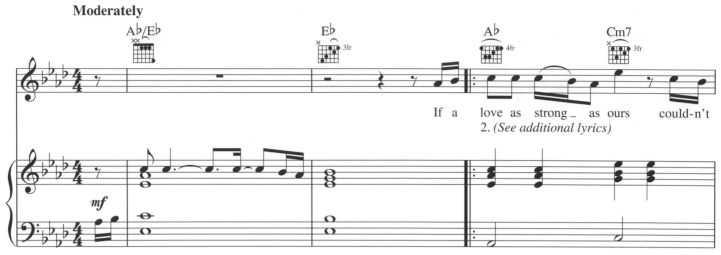

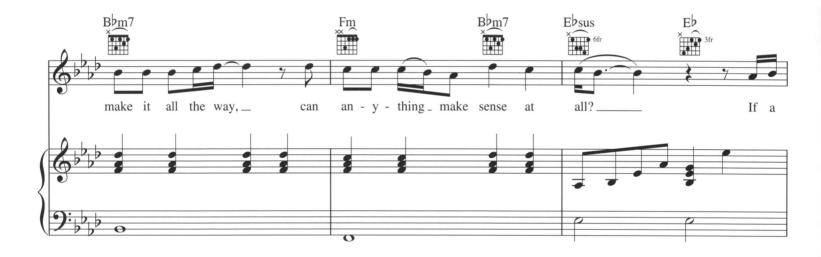

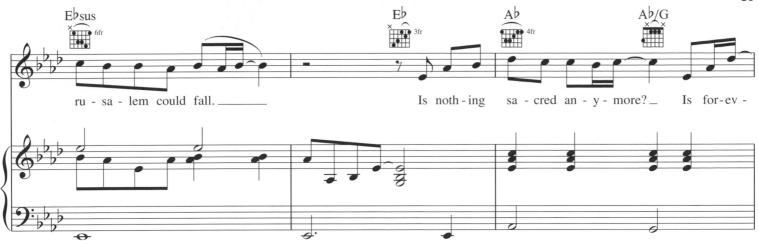

ru - sa - lem could fall. _____ Is noth-ing sa-cred an-y-more? _ Is for-ev-

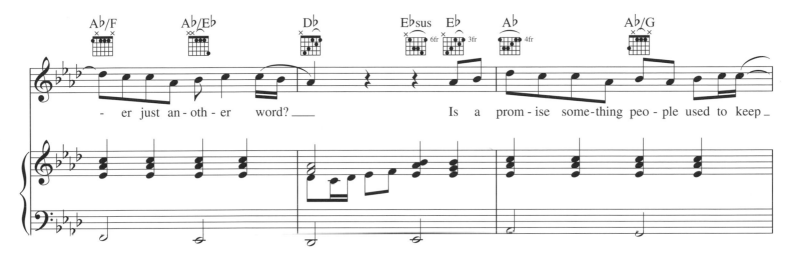

- er just an-oth-er word? ___ Is a prom-ise some-thing peo-ple used to keep _

_____ when love was worth the fight-ing for? _____

__ If we can say _ good-bye, if __ we can say good-bye, _____

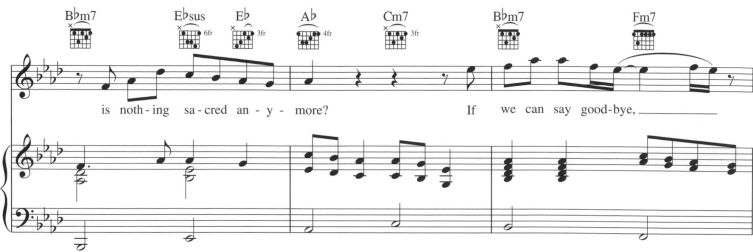

is noth-ing sa-cred an-y-more? If we can say good-bye, _____

is noth-ing sa-cred an-y-more? I've re- more?

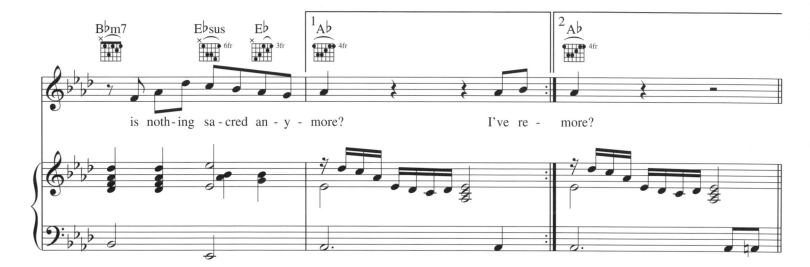

Our love _ was as cer-tain as the dawn, _ as sol-id and safe _ as an-y

love could be. Our love _ was a star you wish up-on, _____ you

thought that I'd save you, I could've sworn that you'd save me. _____ Is noth-ing

sa-cred an-y-more?_ Is for-ev - er just an-oth-er word? _____ Is a

prom-ise some-thing peo-ple used_ to keep _____ when love was worth the fight-ing for?_

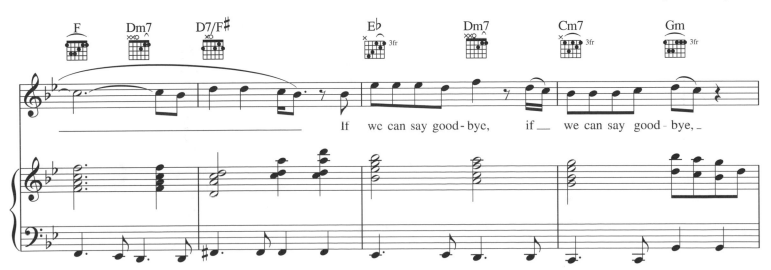

_____ If we can say good-bye, if _ we can say good-bye, _

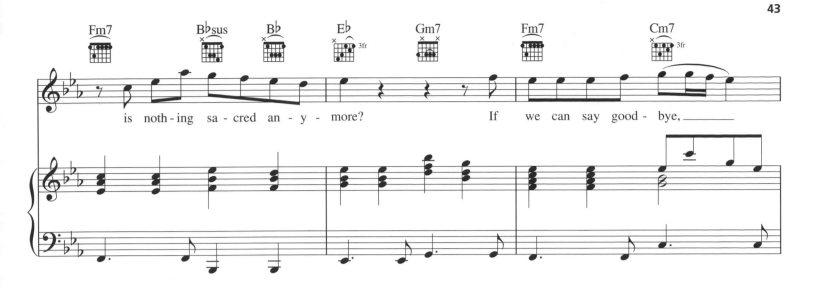

is noth-ing sa-cred an-y-more?   If we can say good-bye,_____

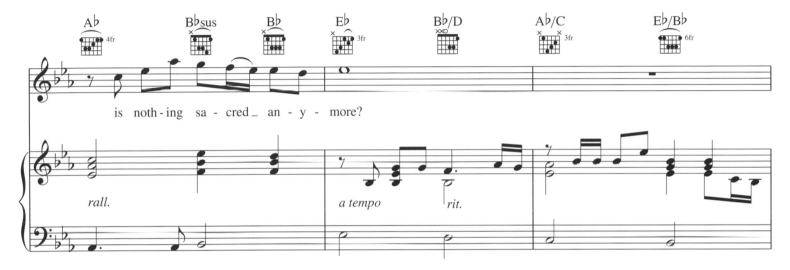

is noth-ing sa-cred__ an-y-more?

rall.   *a tempo*   *rit.*

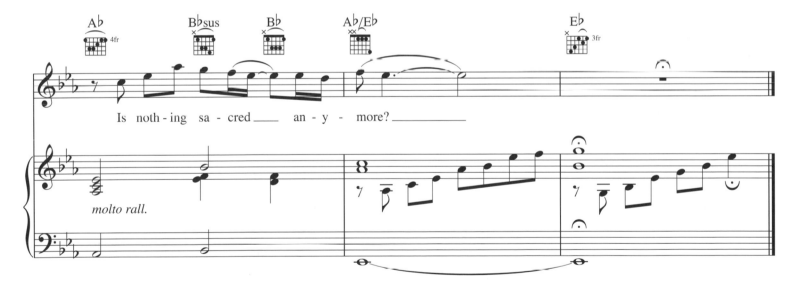

Is noth-ing sa-cred____ an-y-more?____

molto rall.

Additional Lyrics

2. I've relived our final words,
   Every sentence that was said,
   Don't know what turned our lives around.
   Doesn't matter who was right,
   There's no justice in a dream,
   Never thought a heart could break without making any sound.

LOVE CHANGES EVERYTHING

from ASPECTS OF LOVE

Music by ANDREW LLOYD WEBBER
Lyrics by DON BLACK and CHARLES HART

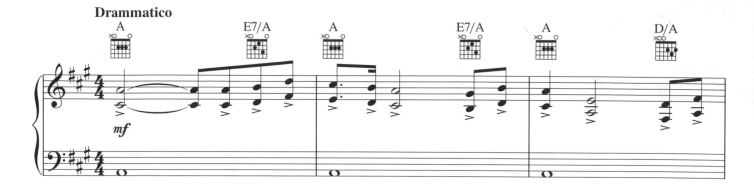

Love,   love chang - es ev - 'ry - thing: hands and
Love,   love chang - es ev - 'ry - thing: days are

fac - es,   earth and sky.   Love,   love chang - es
long - er,   words mean more.   Love,   can break the

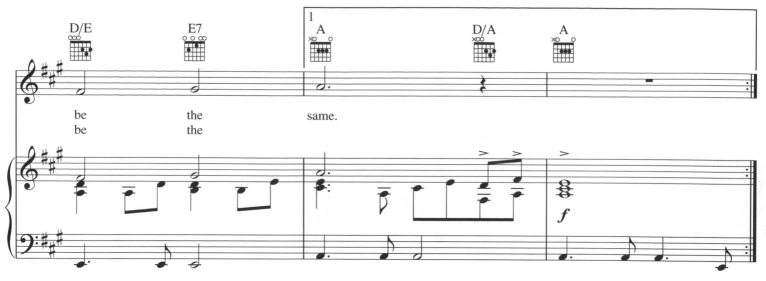

be   the   same.
be   the

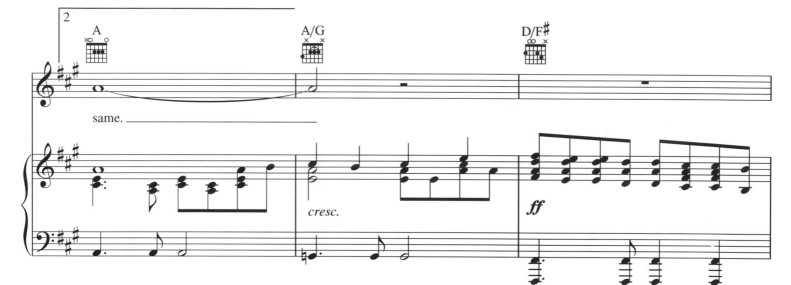

same. _____

cresc.

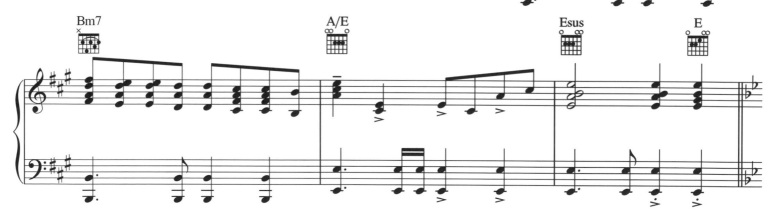

Off _____ in - to the world we go,   plan - ning fu - tures,   shap - ing

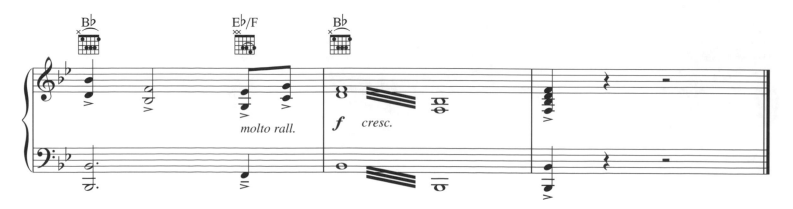

NEXT TIME YOU FALL IN LOVE

from STARLIGHT EXPRESS

Music by ANDREW LLOYD WEBBER
Lyrics by DON BLACK

guess I'm not too good at keep-ing love a - live for long, I
- times you turn a - way from what your heart tells you is right, and

think I've found the ans-wers but the
so you set - tle for what-ev - er

ans-wer's al - ways wrong. My first love was my true love and it should have been my last, the
gets you through the night. The flame you thought was dead may sud-den - ly be - gin to burn, and

on - ly time I'm hap-py's when I'm dream-ing in the past. Next time you fall in love_____
bro-ken hearts can be re-paired, that's some-thing that you learn.

_____ it bet - ter be with me,__ the way it used to be. Back then__

was when__ we touched the star-light. Some -

I've re-lived ev-ery mo-ment that I

ev - er shared with you, what fools we were to end a dream that

looked like com-ing true. Next time you fall in love_____ it bet - ter

be with me,___ the way it used to be. Back then___ was when_

___ we touched the star - light. Next time you

I guess I'm not too good at keep-ing love a - live for long, I

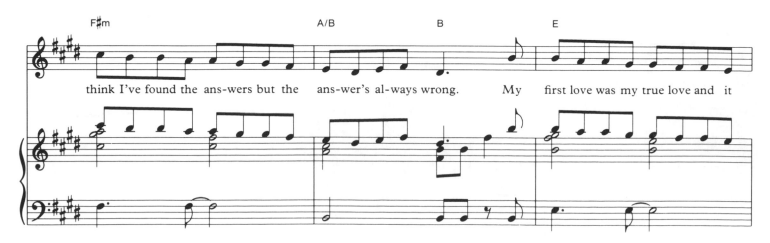

think I've found the ans-wers but the ans-wer's al-ways wrong. My first love was my true love and it

should have been my last, the on-ly time I'm hap-py's when I'm dream-ing in the past. Next time you

fall in love_____ it bet-ter be with me,_ the way it used to be. Back then

1.

_ was when_ we touched the star-light. Next time you

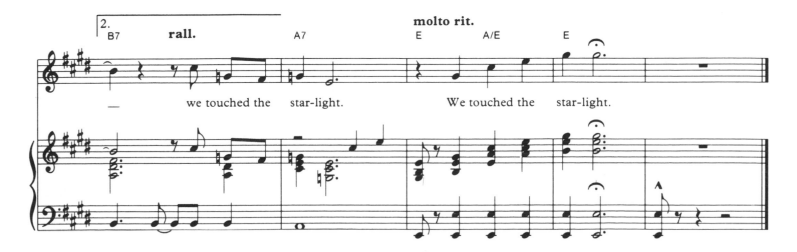

2. **rall.** **molto rit.**

_ we touched the star-light. We touched the star-light.

THE MAN WITH THE GOLDEN GUN

from THE MAN WITH THE GOLDEN GUN

Words by DON BLACK
Music by JOHN BARRY

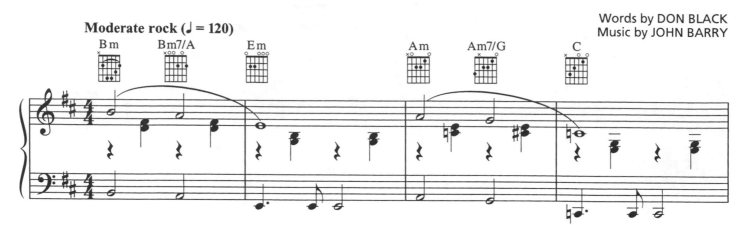

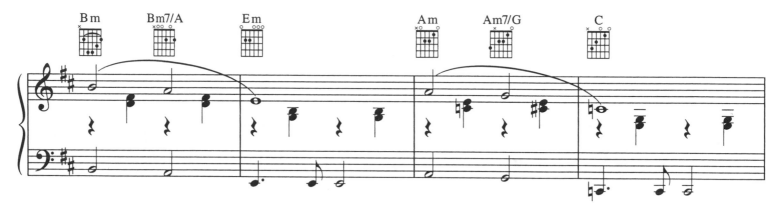

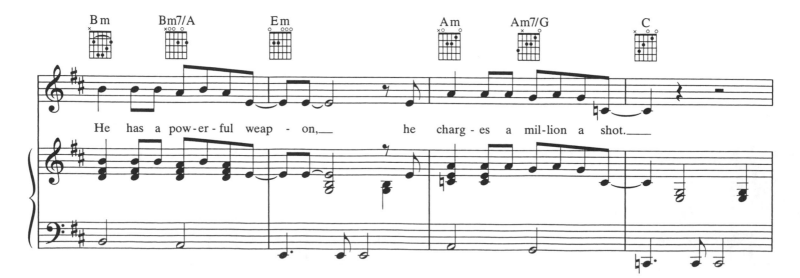

He has a pow-er-ful weap-on,___ he charg-es a mil-lion a shot.___

ON DAYS LIKE THESE

from the Paramount Motion Picture THE ITALIAN JOB

Words by DON BLACK
Music by QUINCY JONES

call the man - y things we left un - said. _____ It's on days like

these _____ that I re - mem - ber, _____ sing - ing songs and drink - ing

wine, while your eyes played games with mine. _____ On days like

these I won - der what be - came of you. _____ May - be to

SAM

Words and Music by DON BLACK,
JOHN FARRAR, and HANK MARVIN

PLEASE DON'T MAKE
ME LOVE YOU

from DRACULA

Words and Music by DON BLACK,
FRANK WILDHORN and CHRISTOPHER HAMPTON

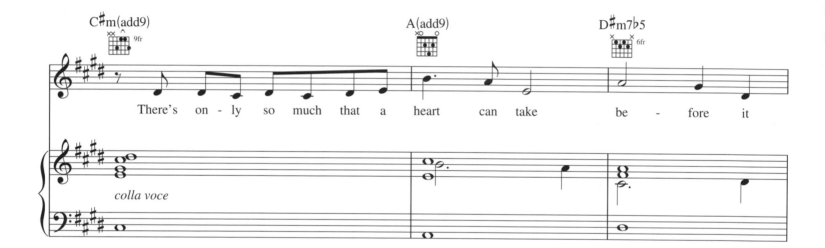

There's on-ly so much that a heart can take be-fore it

starts to break. Please don't make me love you, please don't make me need you.

I've no room in my life for some-thing like this. Please don't take my morn - ings,

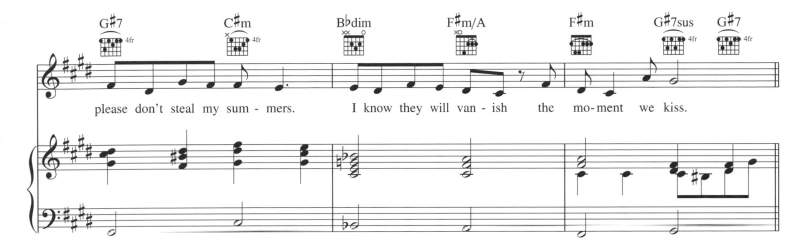

please don't steal my sum - mers. I know they will van - ish the mo - ment we kiss.

I grow weak when we talk, I'm con - fused when we touch.

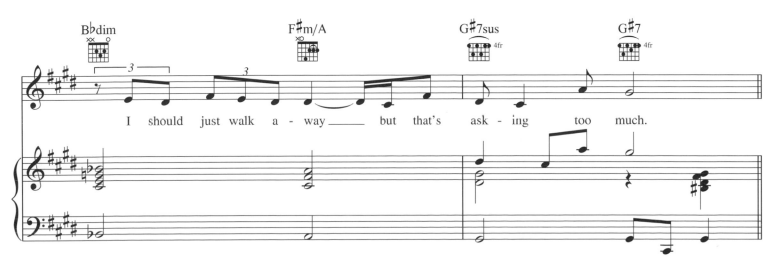

I should just walk a - way _____ but that's ask - ing too much.

Please don't make me do this, please don't make me want this.

All my dreams were tak-en un-til I met you. You're the one I think of

soon as I a-wak-en. Fun-ny how the heart tells the mind what to do. I'm

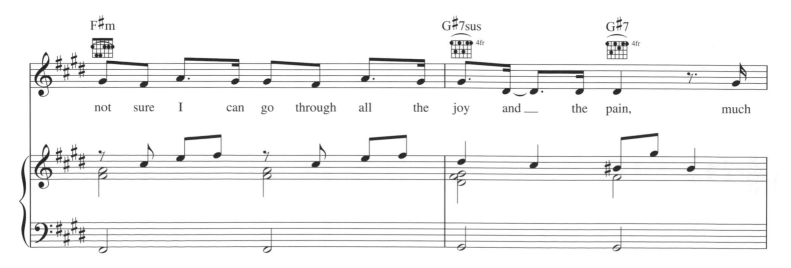

not sure I can go through all the joy and ___ the pain, much

SHAKALAKA BABY

from BOMBAY DREAMS

Words and Music by A.R. RAHMAN,
DON BLACK and MARIUS DE VRIES

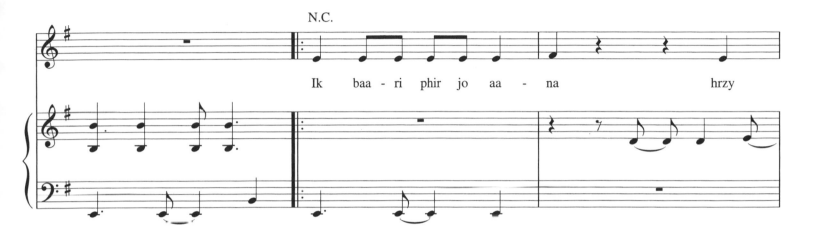

Coda

N.C.

go.　　　　　　Mil - en - ge　jaa - na.

percussion fade out

Verse 2:
In a trance, going out of my mind
You made a flame that keeps me burning
Come on, baby, give me a sign
One word from you and the world stops turning
(Oh, oh, oh) Music is inside me
(Oh, oh, oh, oh) I need you here beside me
(Oh, oh) I know you'll satisfy me
That you are my Bombay lover.
Shakalaka baby, shakalaka baby
This is how it's really meant to be
Shakalaka baby, shakalaka baby
Come and shakalaka with me.
Shakalaka baby, shakalaka baby
I just wanna love you every day
Shakalaka baby, shakalaka baby
Promise me you'll never go away.

Verse 4:
Shakalaka baby, shakalaka baby
This is how it's really meant to be
Shakalaka baby, shakalaka baby
Come and shakalaka with me.
Shakalaka baby, shakalaka baby
Nothing here at all I need to know
Shakalaka baby, shakalaka baby
Now you're here, I'll never let you go.

TELL ME ON A SUNDAY
from SONG AND DANCE

Music by ANDREW LLOYD WEBBER
Lyrics by DON BLACK

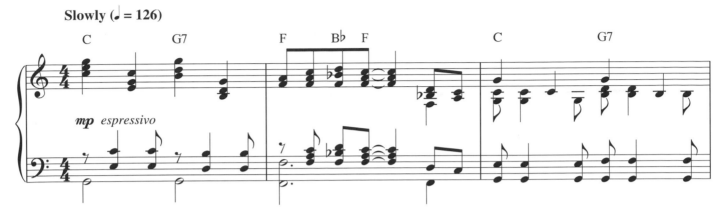

Don't write a let - ter when you want to leave,

don't call me at 3 a. m. from a friend's a - part - ment; I'd like to choose how I

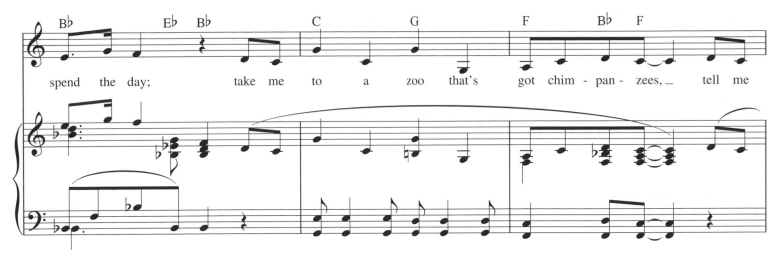

spend the day; take me to a zoo that's got chim-pan-zees, __ tell me

on a Sun-day please. Don't want to know who's to blame,

it won't help know-ing. Don't want to fight day and night, bad e-nough __ you're go-ing.

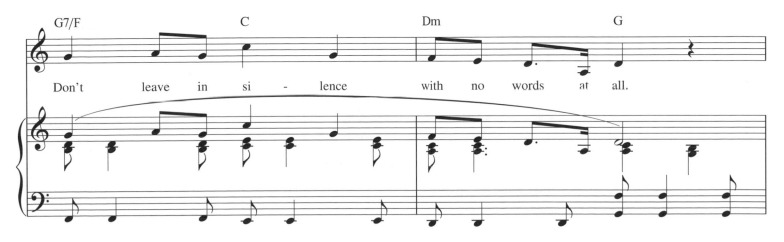

Don't leave in si-lence with no words at all.

Don't get drunk and slam the door; __ that's no way to end this; I know how I want you to

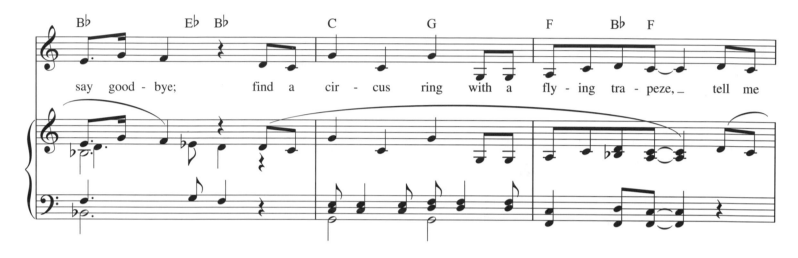

say good - bye; find a cir - cus ring with a fly - ing tra - peze, __ tell me

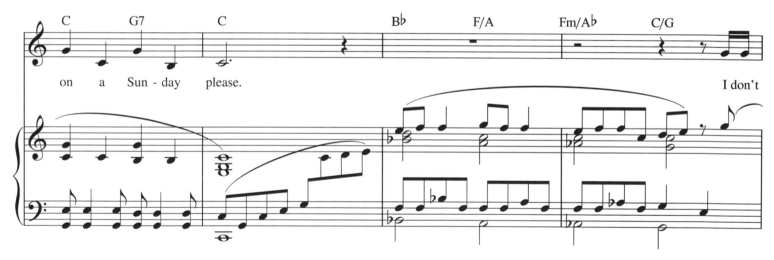

on a Sun - day please. I don't

want to fight day and night; bad e - nough you're go - ing. Don't leave in si - lence

TO SIR, WITH LOVE

from TO SIR, WITH LOVE

Words by DON BLACK
Music by MARC LONDON

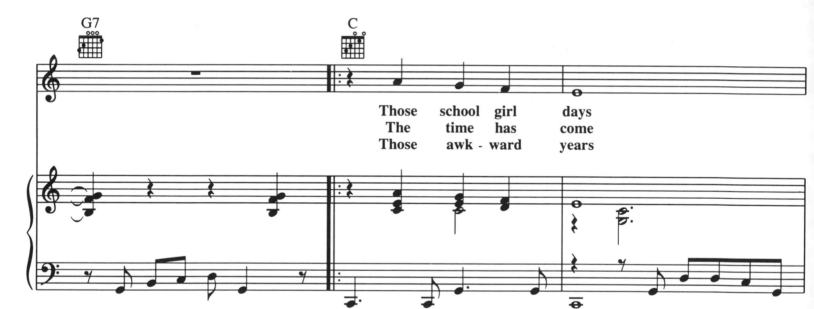

Those school girl days
The time has come
Those awk-ward years

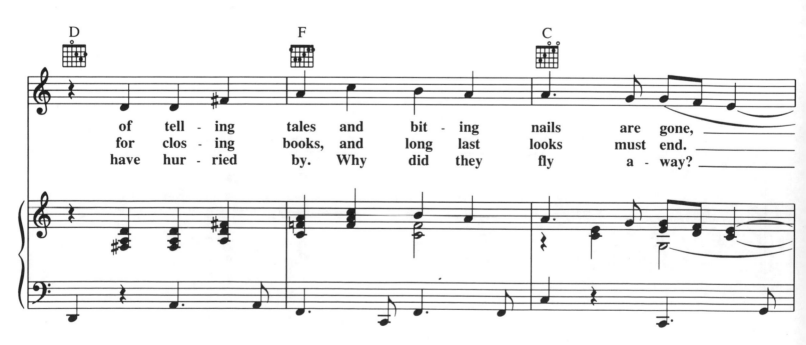

of tell-ing tales and bit-ing nails are gone, ___
for clos-ing books, and long last looks must end. ___
have hur-ried by. Why did they fly a-way? ___

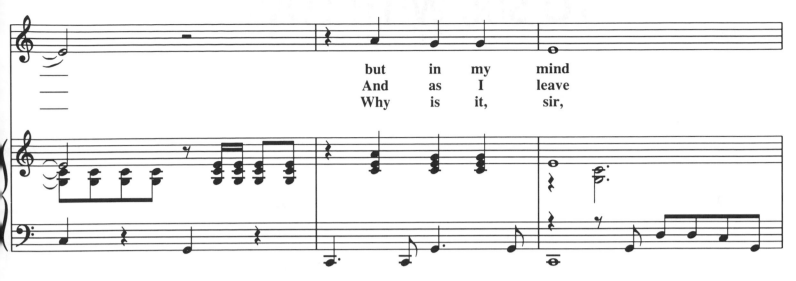

but in my mind
And as I leave
Why is it, sir,

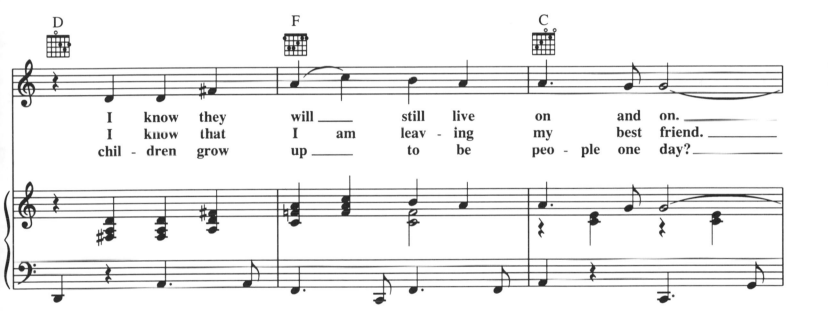

D   F   C

I know they will _____ still live on and on. _____
I know that I am still leav - ing my best friend. _____
chil - dren grow up _____ to be peo - ple one day? _____

B7   Em

But how do you thank some - one _____ who has
A friend who taught me right from wrong _ and
What takes the place of climb - ing trees _____ and

tak - en you from cray-ons to per-fume.
weak from strong, that's a lot to learn.
dir - ty knees in the world out-side?

It is-n't
What! What can I
What is there

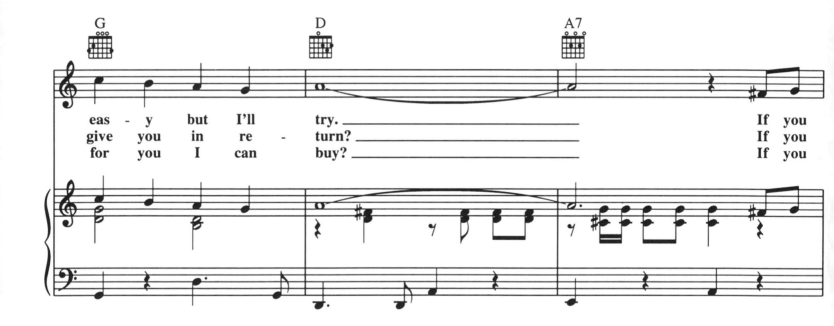

eas - y but I'll try. _____ If you
give you in re - turn? _____ If you
for you I can buy? _____ If you

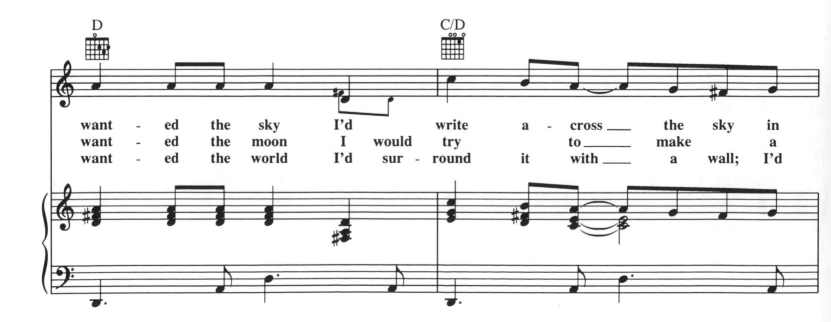

want - ed the sky I'd write a - cross _____ the sky in
want - ed the moon I would try to _____ make a
want - ed the world I'd sur - round it with _____ a wall; I'd

let - ters ____ that would soar a thou - sand feet ____
start, ____ but I would rath - er you let me
scrawl ____ these words with let - ters ten feet

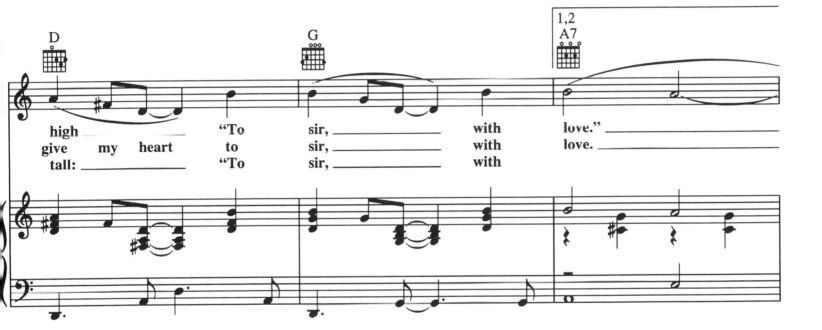

high ____ "To sir, ____ with love." ____
give my heart to sir, ____ with love. ____
tall: ____ "To sir, ____ with

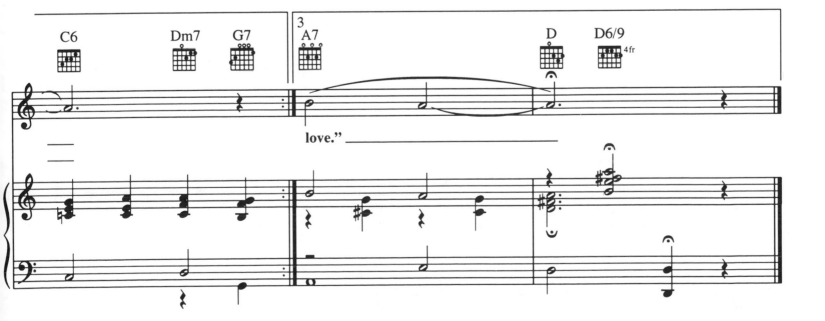

love." ____

TRUE GRIT
Theme from the Paramount Picture TRUE GRIT

Words by DON BLACK
Music by ELMER BERNSTEIN

One day, lit-tle girl, the sad-ness will leave your face _____ as soon as we've won your fight to get jus-tice done.

UNEXPECTED SONG
from SONG AND DANCE

Music by ANDREW LLOYD WEBBER
Lyrics by DON BLACK

Gently ♩=76

I have ne-ver felt like this, for once I'm lost for words, your smile has real-ly
I don't know what's go-ing on can't work it out at all, what-ev-er made you

thrown me. This is not like me at all I ne-ver thought I'd
choose me? I just can't be-lieve my eyes, you look at me as

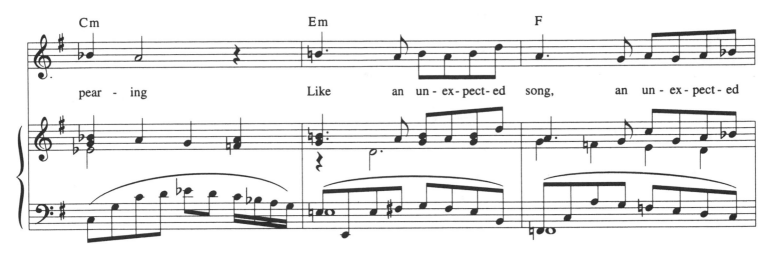

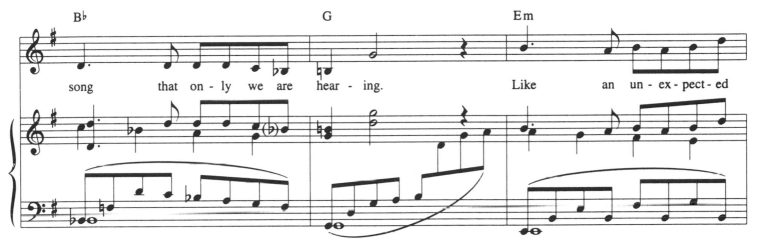

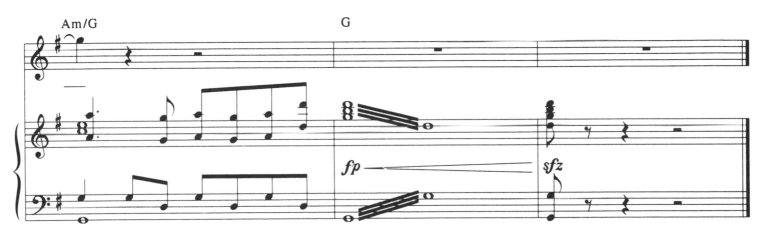

WITH ONE LOOK

from SUNSET BOULEVARD

Music by ANDREW LLOYD WEBBER
Lyrics by DON BLACK and CHRISTOPHER HAMPTON,
with contributions by AMY POWERS

When I speak it's with my soul. I can play a-ny role. No words can tell the stor-ies my eyes tell. Watch me when I frown, you can't write that down. You know I'm right, it's there in black and white. When I look your way you'll hear what I say. Yes,

with one look I put words to shame, just one look sets the screen a-flame.

Si - lent mu-sic starts to play. One tear in my eye makes the whole world cry.

With one look they'll for - give the past, they'll re - joice I've re-turned at last

to my peo-ple in the dark, still out there in the dark.

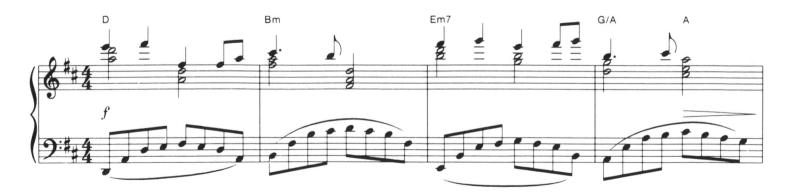

Si - lent mu-sic starts to play. With one look you'll know all you need to know.

With one look I'll ig-nite a blaze, I'll re-turn to my glo-ry days.

They'll say Nor-ma's back at last. This time I am stay-ing, I'm stay-ing for good, I'll be

back where I was born to be. With one look I'll be me.

THE WORLD IS NOT ENOUGH

from the MGM Motion Picture THE WORLD IS NOT ENOUGH

Music by DAVID ARNOLD
Lyrics by DON BLACK

Mysteriously, with a steady pulse

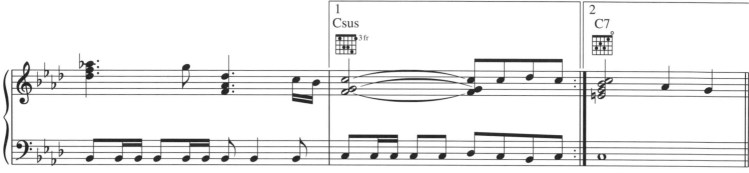

place _ to _ start _ my _ love. And if you're strong e - nough,

to - geth - er we can take the world _ a - part my _ love.

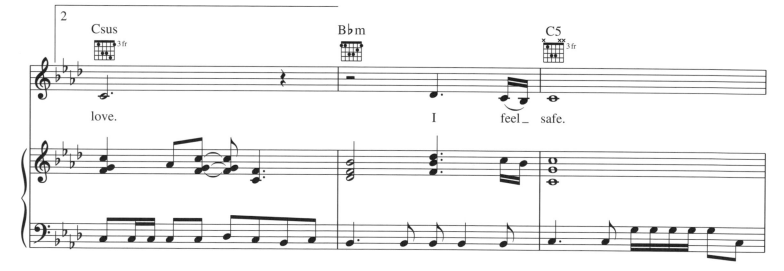

love. I feel _ safe.

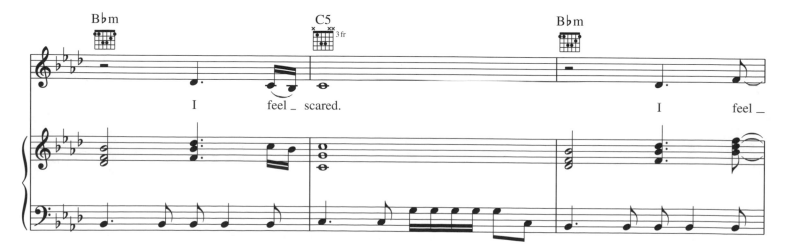

I feel _ scared. I feel _

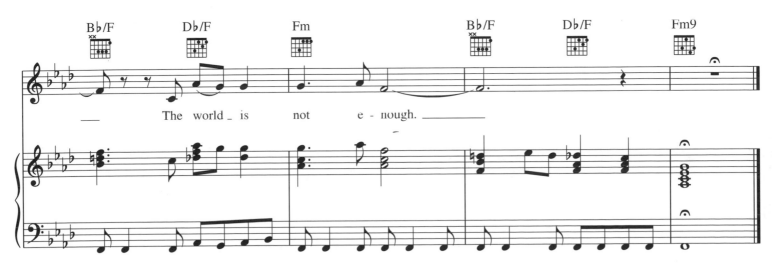

THUNDERBALL
from THUNDERBALL

Words by DON BLACK
Music by JOHN BARRY

Moderately slow (♩ = 92)

1. He al - ways runs when oth - ers walk. He
2. He knows the mean - ing of suc - cess. His

acts while oth - er men just talk._____ He
needs are more so he gives less._____ They

looks at this world and wants it all, so he
call him the win - ner who takes all, and he

*Original recording in B♭ minor.

fight goes on and on and on._____ But he

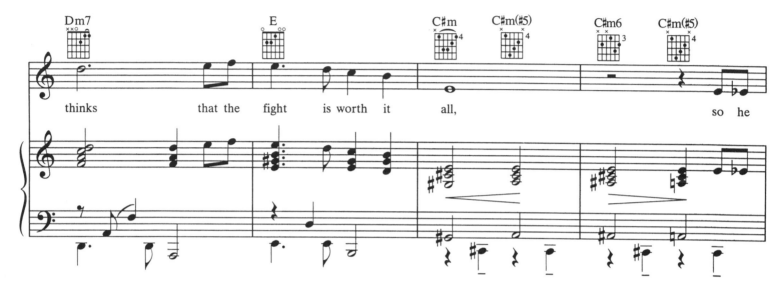

thinks that the fight is worth it all, so he

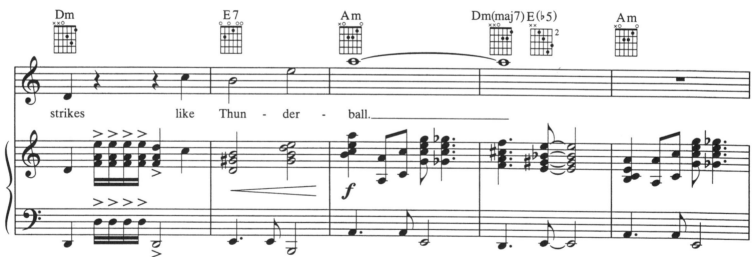

strikes like Thun - der - ball._____

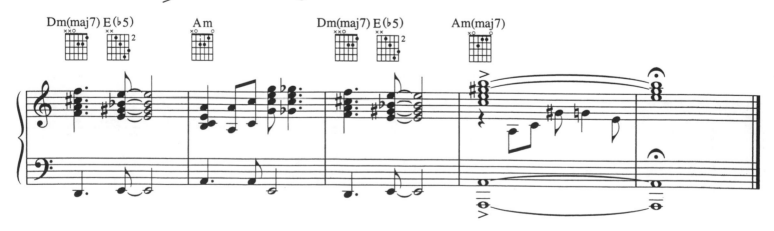